An Appleseed Editions book

First published in 2010 by Franklin Watts
338 Euston Road, London NW1 3BH

Franklin Watts Australia
Hachette Children's Books
Level 17/207 Kent St, Sydney, NSW 2000

© 2010 Appleseed Editions

Created by Appleseed Editions Ltd,
Well House, Friars Hill, Guestling,
East Sussex TN35 4ET

Designed by Helen James
Edited by Mary-Jane Wilkins
Artwork by Graham Rosewarne
Picture research by Su Alexander
Consultant: Steve Parker

ISBN 978 1 4451 0017 3

Dewey Classification 612.8

A CIP catalogue for this book is available from the British Library.

Photograph acknowledgements
page 4 Brigitte Sporrer/Corbis; 7 Michael Keller/Corbis; 8 Omikron/Science Photo Library;
9 Montreal Neurological Institute/Science Photo Library; 12 Steve Gschmeissner/Science
Photo Library; 13 Sovereign, ISM/Science Photo Library; 14 Patrik Giardino/Corbis;
15 Annabella Bluesky/Science Photo Library; 17 Christine Schneider/Corbis; 26 Bryan
and Cherry Alexander/Alamy; 27 Darama/Corbis; 18 Jean-Pierre Lescourret/Corbis;
19 David White/Alamy; 21 Frontline Photography/Alamy; 22 Foodfolio/Alamy;
23 Erich Nguyen/Alamy; 25 LWA-Dann Tardif/Corbis; 28 Simon Marcus/Corbis;
29 A.Inden/Corbis
Front cover Sovereign, ISM/Science Photo Library

Printed in China

Franklin Watts is a division of Hachette Children's Books,
an Hachette UK company.
www.hachette.co.uk

# Contents

# What's around you?

Imagine that you couldn't see the sky or hear a friend's voice. What would it be like if you couldn't smell your favourite meal, or taste a tropical fruit? How could you live without touching people and things? Your senses give you important information about the world around you.

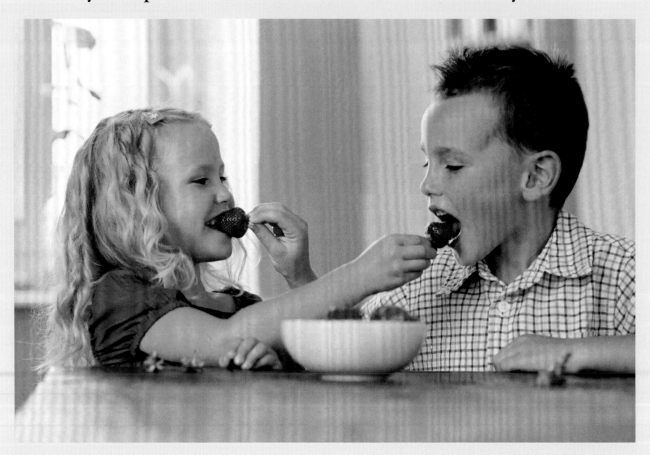

## Five senses

You have five senses that give you lots of details about what's happening around you. Each sense responds to something in the environment. Your eyes respond to light rays and tell you whether the sky is blue or if there are clouds bringing rain. Your ears respond to sound waves and

*We use our sense organs all the time for looking at, hearing, tasting, smelling and touching the things around us.*

tell you about the tone of people's voices – they can tell you whether a voice is a familiar friend's or a stranger's voice.

Your nose detects tiny **molecules** in the air and can pick up the tiniest whiff of a burger on a barbecue, or dog poo on your shoe. The taste buds on your tongue can also detect molecules and tell you how delicious a mango or a strawberry might be. Your sense of touch comes from pressure on nerve endings in your skin, so when you put your arm around your best mate you feel the sense of closeness that only touch can bring.

*This picture shows how important each of our senses is. Our eyes are our most important sense and our lips, hands, tongue and feet are the most sensitive to touch.*

## Losing a sense

Many people do not have all five senses. They may be born without a sense – usually sight or hearing. Sometimes people lose a sense as a result of an illness or because the sense has been damaged. Ears can be harmed by very loud noise and eyes can be damaged by too much **ultraviolet radiation** from the sun. People who lose a sense may find that they can concentrate harder on their other senses. For example, people who lose their sight may learn to listen more carefully.

# A pair of eyes

Your amazing sense of sight, or vision, allows you to do many things. You can catch a ball flying through the air, see a plane in the sky many miles away, read the words in a book and tell the difference between a million colours.

cornea

watery fluid

lens

retina

optic nerve

## A kind of camera

Each of your eyes is like a small ball about 2.5 cm across that sits inside the front of your skull. It has six muscles which allow the eyeball to swivel from side to side and move up and down. Some people can look at their nose and go cross-eyed!

At the front of your eye, the eyeball has three transparent layers: a thin, curved cornea and a **lens** with a little watery fluid

*The retina that lines the inside of the eyeball contains nerve cells that are sensitive to light rays. A nerve called the optic nerve takes messages from these cells to the brain.*

sandwiched between. Together, these layers focus light rays on to the centre of a layer called a **retina** inside the back of the eye. Light rays reflected from an object form an upside-down image on the retina, as if the eye were a kind of camera.

Everyone should visit an **optician** for an eye test from time to time. Opticians can prescribe glasses or contact lenses for people whose eye lenses don't change shape enough – this can make them short- or long-sighted. People who are short-sighted need help to see objects far away. They often wear glasses when they are driving. People who are long-sighted need help to see objects close to them, and they wear glasses to read books or browse the Internet. Opticians can also detect other health problems, such as high **blood pressure**, by looking at the retina at the back of the eye.

## The changing lens

The lens in your eye is stretchy and elastic. Muscles make the lens change shape so that it can focus light rays from objects that are both near and far away. When you try to focus on something several hundred metres away, such as a tree on a hillside or a building on the horizon, the lens becomes flat. When you focus your eyes on a nearby object, such as a page in a book, the lens bulges and becomes more spherical (rounder). This process of changing the shape of the lens is called **accommodation**.

*During an eye test an optician can tell how well your eyes are working by checking the power of each lens to change shape.*

# Looking and seeing

Your eyes are really part of your central nervous system.
They detect the light rays reflected by objects or
given off by lights such as a torch or traffic light,
but it is your brain that does the seeing!

## Rods and cones

The retina of the eye contains
two kinds of nerve cell – called
**rods** and **cones**. They are called
**receptors** and are very sensitive to
light. Rods help you to see things
when the light around you is dim,
for example at night. The cones are
grouped around the centre of the
retina. They work in bright light,
when they allow you to see things
in different colours.

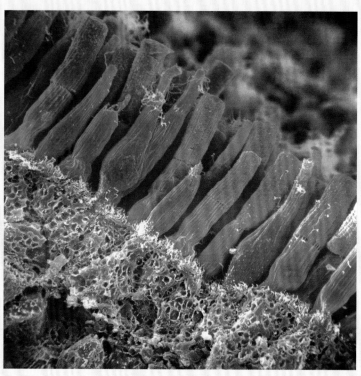

*The retina contains many rods
(green) and cones (blue).*

You
have about
120 million rods
and six million cones
inside the retina
of each eye.

## Seeing with your brain

When light rays fall on the retina,
they activate the rods and cones.
These cells send electrical messages
along the optic nerve from the back
of the eyeball to your brain. This
is where you see the image of the
object you're looking at.

*This brain scan shows what happens when the cells in a part of the brain called the visual cortex (red and white area at the top) are active.*

At the lower rear of your brain is an area called the **visual cortex**. Here, a number of cells put together an image of what you're looking at. Another part of the brain, perhaps your memory, tells you what the object is. You can play tricks called optical illusions with the way your eyes and brain work together and these can make you think you see things that aren't there.

## Three dimensions

Your two eyes set in the front of your head help you see in three dimensions. This gives you **stereoscopic vision**. If you look through just one eye you see things in two dimensions, which means they look flat. Using stereoscopic vision you can see the height, width and depth of an object. So you can see in three dimensions.

Each eye has something called a **field of view**. This is the area in front of you that the eye can see. Your left eye has one and your right eye has a different one. The two fields of view overlap in the centre. Your brain 'sees' objects in this central area in three dimensions, as though you were looking through a pair of binoculars.

*This optical illusion shows you how easy it is to fool your eyes into seeing what's not really there.*

# Inside your ears

You use your eyes more than any other sense, but you rely on your ears to detect the sounds around you. You use your ears to listen to music, hear your phone ringing and tell what your friends are saying.

## Parts of the ear

Your ear has three main parts: outer, middle and inner. The ear you can see is the start of the outer ear. This leads to the eardrum. The other side of the eardrum is the middle ear where you will find the body's three tiniest bones, called the **ossicle bones**. These bones join the eardrum to a thin sheet or **membrane** called the oval window

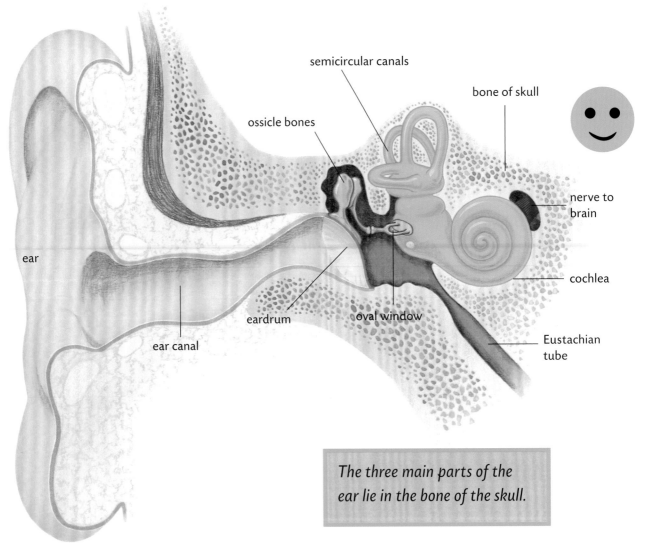

semicircular canals

bone of skull

ossicle bones

nerve to brain

ear

cochlea

eardrum

oval window

ear canal

Eustachian tube

*The three main parts of the ear lie in the bone of the skull.*

**10**

## Did you know?

Your eardrum is about the same size as your smallest fingernail – but much, much thinner.

*Your middle and inner ears are beneath the bones of your face and run below your eyeballs.*

where the **inner ear** begins. The middle and inner parts of your ear are deep inside your skull, which protects them. The middle ear is connected to your nose and your throat by a canal called the **Eustachian tube**.

## The inner ear

Inside your inner ear is the cochlea, which looks like a tiny snail's shell. It is full of fluid, as well as millions of tiny hairs and two very sensitive membranes. This is where sounds from the outside world are turned into nerve signals that go to the brain. Next to the cochlea are three loops called semicircular canals. These canals are very important in helping you to keep your balance (see pages 14-15).

## WHAT IS SOUND?

The sounds you hear are **vibrations** moving through the air as waves. When the waves are bunched up tightly you hear a high sound. The amount of bunching up is called the **frequency**. The more the waves are bunched up, the higher the frequency and the higher the sound or the **pitch**. Waves which are spread out have a lower frequency and a lower pitch.

# Hearing and listening

Sounds make vibrations which travel through
the parts of your ear and are turned into nerve signals.
Your brain then interprets these signals and identifies
the sound – for example, the bark of a dog,
the crash of a wave or the horn of a car.

*When the tiny hair cells (red) in the
cochlea of the inner ear move in the
fluid they send messages to the brain.*

## Moving waves

The waves from a sound enter your ear, where they move along the ear canal and set the eardrum vibrating. These sound vibrations are picked up by the three ossicle bones and passed on to the oval window of the inner ear.

As the oval window vibrates it moves the fluid in the cochlea at the same frequency as the original sound that entered your outer ear. This vibrates the membranes and hair cells inside the cochlea (see above), which send messages as nerve signals to your brain. This part of the brain, called the auditory cortex, decodes the signals and hears the exact pitch and loudness of the sound.

## Where's that sound?

Your brain can tell exactly which direction a sound is coming from and how far away it is. Having two ears helps. A sound exactly in front of you or behind you reaches both ears at the same time. However, a sound on one side of you takes a fraction of a second longer to reach the ear on the other side of you.

The brain can automatically work out where the sound is coming from because of this tiny difference.

*When we listen to words, the cells in the auditory cortex part of the brain and an area just behind it (shown in red and green) are active.*

# Keeping your balance

Inside each of your inner ears is a structure which helps you to keep your balance. This is why you don't fall over when you move. The structure detects every movement your head makes and tells your brain how to change the position of your body.

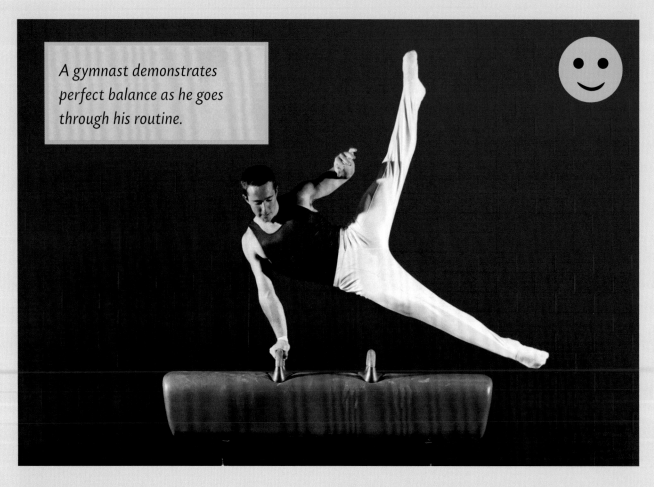

A gymnast demonstrates perfect balance as he goes through his routine.

## Hair cells

The structure is called a **vestibule** and it is connected to the cochlea (see pages 12-13). Each vestibule has three curving canals and two spaces which are filled with a fluid that moves when your head moves. They also have tiny, delicate hair cells that bend when the fluid moves around them. When the hair cells bend, they send nerve signals to the brain.

The hair cells can sense when you are moving in one direction – for example, riding in a train or going up and down in a lift. They can also sense the force of gravity, which helps you understand which way is up – for example, when you find yourself in total darkness.

## Detecting movements

The curving semicircular canals in both ears enable you to know the position of your head at any time. When you turn your head, the fluid and hair cells inside one canal sense the movement. If you spin round and round, you start to feel giddy and lose your balance. This is because the fluid and hair cells in all three canals are trying to tell you where your head is. If you do lose your balance and fall over, the fluid and hair cells take a little while to settle down again.

*A teenage girl uses an audiometer to test the sensitivity of her hearing.*

## HEALTH CHECK
## Hearing tests

People who are having difficulty with their hearing can have two kinds of test. The first test looks at the eardrum and the bones of each middle ear. If these are working normally, the doctor will perform a second test, called **audiometry**, to find out if there is a problem in the inner ear. The person listens to a sound at a particular frequency – soft at first, then gradually growing louder. The person presses a button when he or she can hear the sound. This test is done at different frequencies and helps the doctor work out how much hearing a patient has lost and what the cause might be.

# What's up your nose?

You mainly use your nose to breathe. Most of your nose is used to clean and warm the air before it enters your lungs. Only a small part has a sense of smell. This detects some of the molecules in the air.

## Breathing in...

When you breathe deeply through your nose the air goes up through your nostrils into two spaces called **nasal cavities**. Inside are lots of small hairs called **cilia** (say 'silly-a'), which push **mucus** towards the back of your throat to be swallowed. This mucus takes out bacteria and dust from the air before the air goes into your lungs.

At the top of each nasal cavity just beneath the bridge of your nose is a small area called a cleft. A small patch of tissue here is sensitive to many of the molecules in the air. Inside the tissue are millions and millions of tiny sensory hair cells connected to cells called receptors.

*More than 20 million tiny hair cells line the top of the cleft of your nose. They are connected to your olfactory bulb just above. The hair cells detect smell molecules in the air.*

olfactory bulb

cleft

sensitive hair

nose

movement of air

nasal cavity

## Detecting smells

The air contains lots of different molecules. Some of these are picked up by the sensory hair cells, which make the receptor cells produce nerve signals. These go to a part of your brain called the **olfactory bulb**. One bulb sits above each nasal cavity and sorts out all the nerve signals about smells before they are sent on to the smell centre in your brain.

### SNIFFING

When you breathe in through your nose, not much air reaches the cleft at the top of each nostril. When you sniff, you speed up the air so more enters the cleft and touches the sensitive hair cells. This gives you a better chance of smelling what's in the air.

*A woman moves her nose close to a newly opened rose to sniff its fragrance.*

*Air travels slowly through your nose during a normal breath and spreads through the nasal cavity (opposite). When you sniff to smell something (right), the air travels faster and more reaches the sensitive hairs at the top.*

olfactory bulb

cleft

sensitive hair

nose

nasal cavity

movement of air

# Why smell is important

Think of all the smells that might float in the air around you – cooking bacon, freshly-cut grass, the scent of a flower, peeled oranges, unwashed feet, boiled cabbage or sour milk. The huge variety of smells you can detect show you just how important your nose is!

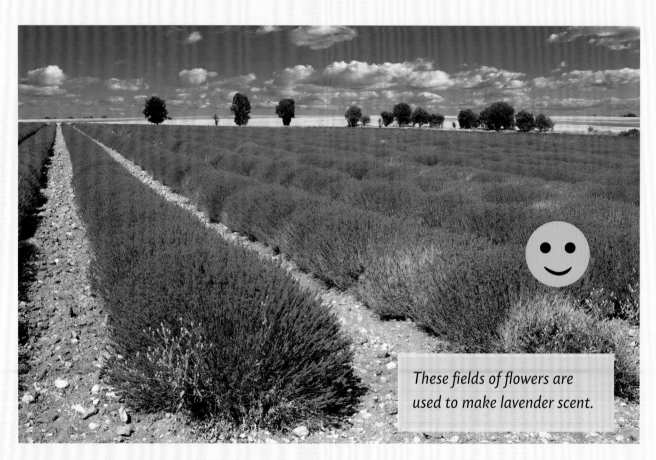

*These fields of flowers are used to make lavender scent.*

## Different kinds of smell

The tiny sensory hairs connected to the olfactory bulb at the top of your nose can detect many different smells. So your sense of smell is more sensitive than your sense of taste (see pages 20-23). Some smells, such as lavender, are stronger than others. This is because they have the lightest molecules. Heavy molecules, such as candlewax, don't smell nearly as strongly.

You use your sense of smell in various ways. Bad smells tell you that something is rotten – for example, milk that has gone sour or butter that is rancid. The bad smell stops you putting the food in your mouth

## SMELLING SALTS

Smelling salts were very popular in the nineteenth century. British policemen carried them to revive people who fainted. When someone loses consciousness they can be revived by opening a small bottle of smelling salts under their nose. The salts release a chemical called ammonia, which irritates the lining of the nasal cavity and makes the lungs inhale hard.

and becoming ill from eating it. Pleasant smells help you to appreciate your food. The aroma of good food wakes up your appetite and makes you realize how hungry you are. Warning smells, such as smoke or petrol, tell you to beware of danger. Other smells are designed to attract other people's attention, for example, perfume or aftershave.

**WHEN THINGS GO WRONG**

## Loss of smell

Your sense of smell works best when you are young, and it becomes less sensitive as you grow older. Some people are born without a sense of smell. When you have a cold, or have an allergic reaction to something such as pollen, the entrance to the nasal cleft is blocked by mucus and you may lose your sense of smell for a day or two.

*The bad smells from rotting food can be very strong. They are usually caused by bacteria breaking down the food.*

# On your tongue

Your sense of taste is similar to your sense of smell, except it comes from your tongue instead of your nose. The two senses often work together because they both detect chemicals in food and drink. Between them they send your brain messages which tell it which food and drinks you really like and which you can't bear.

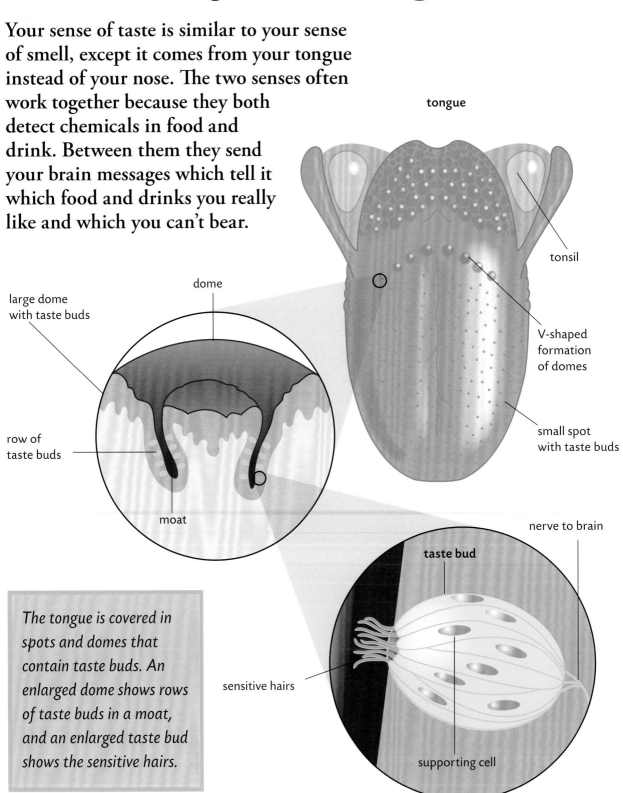

tongue

tonsil

V-shaped formation of domes

small spot with taste buds

large dome with taste buds

dome

row of taste buds

moat

nerve to brain

taste bud

sensitive hairs

supporting cell

*The tongue is covered in spots and domes that contain taste buds. An enlarged dome shows rows of taste buds in a moat, and an enlarged taste bud shows the sensitive hairs.*

*Licking ice cream with your tongue is the best way to enjoy the flavour.*

## Spots and domes

Your tongue is an amazing **organ** made up of muscles that let you chew, swallow, suck and talk. Stick out your tongue in front of a mirror and you will probably see some small domes, spots and pimples on the top. Some of these are used when licking and chewing, and are not involved in taste.

If you look closely you should see larger, round spots in the middle of your tongue. Each spot contains lots of microscopic taste buds. There are tissues that contain taste buds along both sides of your tongue, too, with more of them towards the back. Right at the back and in the middle of your tongue there's a V-shaped formation of between 7 and 12 dome shapes. Each contains about 250 taste buds.

## Lots of layers

A taste bud contains a group of cells that make it look a bit like the layers of an onion. A bunch of sensitive hairs stick out of the bud (see left). Chemicals in your saliva **stimulate** the hairs and the cells, then send a pattern of nerve signals to your brain. Your brain decides what the taste is and whether or not you like it.

### HOW MANY TASTE BUDS?

You have around 10,000 taste buds on your tongue. When you were a baby you probably had some taste buds in your cheeks and on the roof of your mouth, too. Girls tend to have more taste buds than boys.

### Did you know?

A cat's tongue has bigger domes and spots than a human tongue. When cats lick and clean their fur, you can hear a rasping sound.

# Tasting food and drink

We can all detect four or even five different types of taste sensation. As you grow older, the way you taste food and drink can change, which means that you may begin to like some food or drink that you once couldn't face.

## Four types

When we chew a mouthful of food or sip a drink, we use at least four types of taste to help us identify it. These are sweet, sour, salty and bitter. There may even be a fifth 'savoury' taste (see page 23). Every taste, whether it's chocolate, hamburger, cabbage, lemonade, ice cream or fish, is more or less a combination of the four basic taste sensations.

Sugar, honey and **saccharin** are sweet sensations. Vinegar, orange juice and lemon juice give us sour sensations. We all recognize salty sensations. Coffee, unsweetened chocolate, olives and tonic water create bitter tastes.

All areas of your tongue can detect types of taste, although some areas seem to be more sensitive than others to particular sensations.

## Not just taste

Taste buds are not the only parts of your mouth that give you information about food and drink. The top and bottom of your tongue, the lining of your cheeks, the roof and floor of your mouth – and even your gums – are covered with tiny nerve endings that are sensitive to touch. They can tell whether food is hot or cold, hard or soft, smooth or lumpy, and many other sensations.

*Freshly chopped parsley can add flavour to many dishes.*

*Huge piles of spices for sale at a grocer's shop in India.*

People have been adding herbs, spices and seasonings to food for a very long time. The extra flavours added during cooking vary from region to region around the world and they help to stimulate our taste buds.

## Loss of taste

Imagine what it would be like if you couldn't taste anything at all, especially if you lost your sense of smell as well. You might lose interest in food and drink altogether. Problems with the sense of taste can be caused by taking some medicines or by a lack of vitamins. People who smoke, or who are exposed to certain chemicals – or even radiation – can lose their sense of taste.

### A FIFTH TASTE?

Some experts think that there is a fifth taste sensation. It is called umami, which means something like yummy, and it is linked to the savoury flavours in foods. Some foods that make you taste the umami sensation are beef, lamb, soy sauce and parmesan cheese.

# Sensing with your skin

Your skin covers the whole of the outside of your body and it is very sensitive to pain, vibrations, touch and changes in the temperature around you. This sensitivity comes from millions of tiny nerve cells.

## Inside your skin

Your skin has three main layers. On the outside is the epidermis and on the inside is a layer of fat. In between is the dermis, which contains blood vessels, hairs and sweat glands. It also has glands that produce a waxy, oily substance called sebum. This waterproofs your skin.

In addition there are millions of tiny nerve cells that send signals to your brain with information about the outside world.

## Sensing touch

Right at the top of the dermis, where it meets the epidermis, there are sensory nerve endings which are sensitive to light

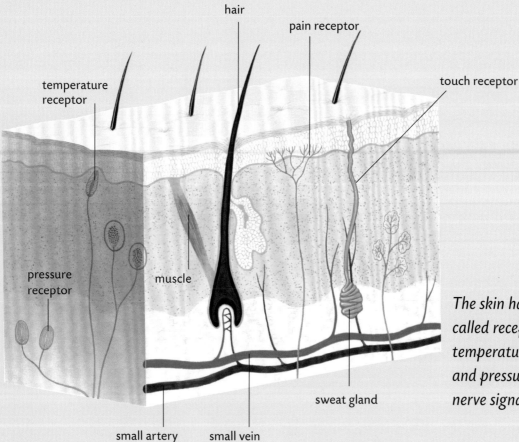

temperature receptor

hair

pain receptor

touch receptor

pressure receptor

muscle

sweat gland

small artery

small vein

*The skin has sensory cells called receptors which feel temperature, pain, touch and pressure. They send nerve signals to the brain.*

touch, such as a kiss on the cheek or a pat on the back. Also at the top of the dermis are nerve endings which detect vibrations like those created by drums in a rock band or by a truck driving by your home.

Nerve cells deeper in the dermis detect much stronger pressure on the skin. These cells are in the palms of your hands, on the soles of your feet, and on your lips, eyelids and nipples. In the palm of your hand, these pressure receptor cells work when you grip something tightly, such as the bar of a roller coaster.

## HOW MANY NERVE CELLS?

Most of the sensory nerve cells in your skin let you feel pain (see pages 26-27). In one square centimetre of skin there are around 200 of these cells, compared with just 15 that feel pressure, six that detect cold and only one that detects warmth. Your fingertips probably have the most sensory nerve cells, and your lower back has the fewest.

*Touch is an important way to show affection, as parents and their children often do.*

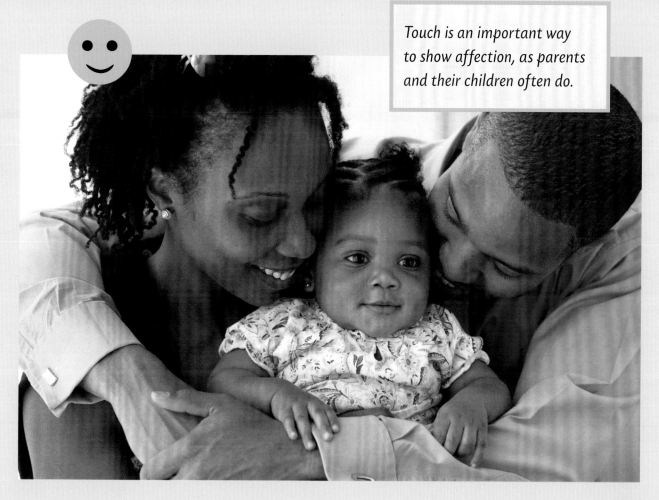

# Feeling temperature and pain

If you dip your finger into a cup of very cold water you quickly realize that all the sensory nerve cells in your skin work together. It's hard to tell which sense works fastest: the touch of the water, or the cold that makes you want to take out your finger.

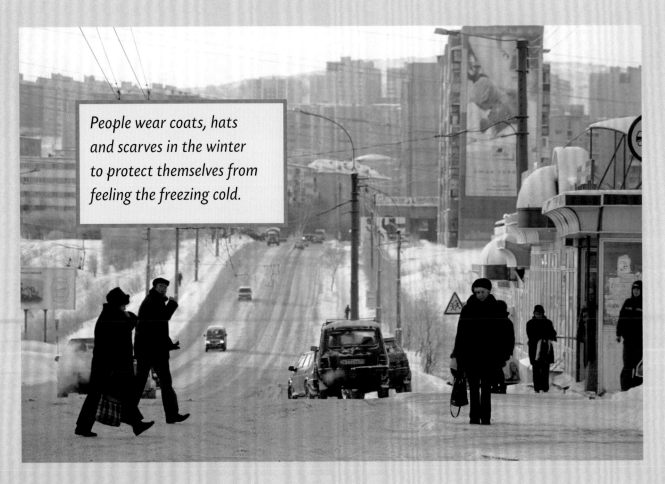

People wear coats, hats and scarves in the winter to protect themselves from feeling the freezing cold.

## Hot and cold

Your skin has special nerve cells which detect the temperature of something placed near it or against it. Some cells detect warmth, while others detect cold.

They allow you to feel the heat from a fire or the chill of a winter wind, the warmth of hot bath water or the cold of an ice cube dropped down your neck.

## Pain in the brain

Headaches and migraines affect many people around the world. Research shows that half of 7- to 15-year-olds get headaches, and 10 per cent of this age group suffer from migraines.

*The pain-detecting cells in this cook's hand sent a message to her brain when she was splashed by boiling water.*

These temperature-sensitive cells warn you about the dangers around you. Together with the cells that detect pain they send nerve signals from your skin, telling the brain how close you are to something very hot or cold. This warning system helps to stop you hurting yourself.

## Ouch!

You feel pain from many sources, such as toothache, a headache, a twisted ankle, a broken bone, a disease that damages your body's tissues – and even if someone pinches or slaps you.

When you feel pain, your body is telling you that something is wrong. Some pain doesn't last long and goes away if you take a painkiller such as aspirin or paracetamol. Other pain can last a long time and can be very distressing.

The sensory nerve cells which register pain are all over your body, not just in your skin. Your tongue and eyes have lots of pain cells, but your insides do not have very many.

When something triggers the cells they send urgent messages to the spinal cord and the brain saying 'Ouch! That hurts!' until the brain does something about it.

# Do you have a sixth sense?

Some people believe we have an extra sense that gives us information about events in the world in addition to our five other senses. It is difficult to prove scientifically that we have a sixth sense, but some especially sensitive people may have it.

*Identical twins seem to have a sixth sense because one often knows what the other is thinking.*

## Extra sense

Have you ever had a strong feeling that you know what someone is thinking, even though they haven't told you? Or have you ever sensed that something is about to happen before it does happen? If you have, you might have experienced a moment of **extrasensory perception**, or ESP.

One ESP power is called **telepathy**. This involves communicating with someone else without actually speaking to them. It's almost as though one brain is talking to another person's brain – a bit like a radio transmitter sending information via waves to a radio receiver.

## Seeing into the future

Another ESP power is called clairvoyancy. This is a process through which someone can see into the future or dream about an event that is about to happen. There are many stories of people who avoid a disaster, such as a plane crash, because they have been warned about it in a dream.

## Gut feeling

Intuition is another part of having a sixth sense. Some people call this having a hunch or a gut feeling. It means you feel or know that something is true or right, even when you don't have a good reason

### SEEN IT BEFORE

People sometimes say, 'I knew that was going to happen' when they see an event taking place. This doesn't mean they have experienced extrasensory perception. This sensation is called déjà vu (day-jar-voo), which is French for 'already seen'. What it means is that the brain can see something and then convince itself that it had seen it before, all in the blink of an eye.

for it. Those who have good powers of intuition do not seem to rely on their ordinary senses as much as other people.

Fortune tellers claim they can tell your future, but this is very unlikely to be true!

# Glossary

**accommodation**    The way the lens of the eye changes shape when it focuses rays of light inside the eye.

**audiometry**    A test that measures how well the ears hear various sounds.

**blood pressure**    The pressure of the blood against the walls of the arteries.

**cilia**    Tiny hairs in the lining of the nasal cavity and other body parts.

**cones**    Special cells, or receptors, in the retina that detect coloured light.

**Eustachian tube**    A canal linking the middle ear with the throat. The Eustachian tube helps to stop pressure building up in the middle ear.

**extrasensory perception (ESP)**    The ability to sense something in the world around you without using any of your five senses.

**field of view**    The area in front of you that one of your eyes can see.

**frequency**    The number of times a sound wave vibrates in a second.

**infection**    A disease caused by an invading organism.

**inner ear**    Part of the ear where sounds are turned into nerve impulses and where the body's position and balance are detected.

**lens**    The transparent part of the eye that focuses light rays on the retina.

**membrane**    A very thin layer inside or around a cell, or a protective covering for a row of cells or larger body part.

**molecules**    The smallest amount of a chemical substance, such as oxygen.

**mucus**    A liquid made by the body to stop membranes from drying out.

**nasal cavity**    The space inside a nostril in the nose.

**olfactory bulb**    The organ of smell at the top of the nasal cavity.

**optician**    A specialist who tests eyes and makes glasses and contact lenses.

**organ**    A major part of the body that has one or more special tasks. The eyes, ears, heart and lungs are all organs.

**ossicle bones**    The three tiny bones found in the middle ear.

**pitch**    The frequency of a sound when it is heard by the ears. The pitch of a sound describes how high or low the frequency is.

**pus**    The thick yellow liquid that forms in an infected wound.

**radiation**    Rays of energy produced by something, such as the sun, a light bulb or a radio transmitter.

**receptors**    Sensory cells that detect something in the world around them.

**retina**   A layer of cells that lines the inside of the eye and is sensitive to light. The retina contains special cells called rods and cones.

**rods**   Special cells, or receptors, in the retina of an eye that allow you to see light, but not colours. Rods help you to see in dim light.

**saccharin**   A manmade chemical for sweetening food and drinks.

**stereoscopic vision**   Seeing in three dimensions using both eyes.

**stimulate**   If you want to make something active you stimulate it.

**telepathy**   A type of extrasensory perception in which two or more people communicate directly without using the five senses.

**ultraviolet**   A type of high-energy radiation produced by the sun.

**vestibule**   Part of the organ of balance found in the inner ear.

**vibrations**   Regular, repeated movements of a substance such as air.

**visual cortex**   The place at the back of the brain where nerve signals from the retina in each eye are turned into images.

# Books

*Human Body* Richard Walker, Dorling Kindersley 2004
*The Oxford Children's A to Z of the Human Body* Bridget
and Neil Ardley, OUP 2003
*Complete Book of the Human Body* Anna Claybourne,
Usborne Publishing 2006
*Eyes: Injury, Illness and Health* and other titles on the senses
*(Body Focus series)* Carol Ballard, Heinemann Library 2009

# Websites

**www.cyh.com/HealthTopics/HealthTopicDetailsKids.
aspx?p=335&np=152&id=1430**
Find out more about your hearing, looking after your ears
and what happens when your ears are infected.

**www.exploringnature.org/**
Find out more about the eyes, ears and other senses.